How To Be A

Zen Mama

13 Ways To Stop Worrying, Let Go And

Be Closer To Your Kids

How To Be A

Zen Mama

13 Ways To Stop Worrying, Let Go And

Be Closer To Your Kids

by Betsy McKee Henry

Zen Mama Publishing

Denver, Colorado

Cover Design by Betsy McKee Henry

Cover Photo by Elizabeth Feldman

Library of Congress Card Number - pending
Henry, Betsy McKee
How to be zen mama: 13 way to stop worrying, let go and
be closer to your kids/Betsy Henry
ISBN 1448674387
1st Edition

This is

dedicated to the

Original Zen Mama,

my mother, Barbie McKee

*"Life is not a problem to be solved,
it is a gift to be opened."*
~Wayne Mulle

TABLE OF CONTENTS

How To Be A

Zen Mama

"If you've had a happy childhood,
no one can ever take that away.
If you've had an unhappy childhood,
you'll search for it the rest of your life.
Give your children a happy childhood.
Treasure your children."
~the Zen Mama

Preface

*"When the student is ready,
the teacher will appear."*
~Zen Proverb

The idea for this book was conceived on a trip to Boulder, Colorado. My husband and I had just finished a challenging year with two of our three children; grades had fallen, limits were being tested. The teenage years are not easy, as anyone with even one teenage child will tell you. Being a positive and optimistic person, I tried to find the lessons in all of our experiences and understand where we had made mistakes. I couldn't continue to be the person I'd become over the summer and the new school year. I was a frantic, nagging mother worried about my kids in this modern world with text messaging and Facebook and our demanding culture that wants them to be volunteers, super athletes and ivy league students. Yet, at my job as a preschool teacher, I felt more Zen-like, giving out pearls of wisdom to those overly concerned parents of my 3-5 year old kids. I decided at that point that I had my own life to live and needed to let my children live their lives. If I let go, maybe we'd all be happier. I decided to combine the two ideas the frantic mother and the Zen like teacher and become one, become a "Zen Mama".

Hopefully this book will be a teacher for you. None of us brings a child into this world with a degree in parenting. I have at times been thankful for my teaching degree, having studied and practiced teaching before having children. But I've also been at a loss more times than I can think! I've worried so much. I've been angry. I've been disappointed. **Emotions like worry, anger and disappointment are habits, and like other bad habits, these can be broken.**

Zen Buddhists learn in life by studying lessons with a master. However, the master will always tell his/her students that she is not really a Zen master, but a student just like them. The Zen Master has just traveled down the road a little further than the students. Read these lessons, and hopefully they will help you when you're worried and need to change your parenting style or your attitude.

Oh, and by the way, you can apply these lessons to other parts of your life: Zen Wife, Zen Daughter, Zen Sister, Zen Friend, Zen Co-worker...you get the picture!

"In youth we learn; in age we understand."
~Marie Ebner-Eschenbach

Introduction To
Buddha And Zen

"All that we are is the result of what we have thought.
The mind is everything. What we think we become."
~Buddha

Many people today talk about Buddha and the practice of Zen without really knowing the details. I know I did. When I started this project I called myself a "Zen Mama" because I was letting go of many of the ways that caused my children and me to suffer. So, I did a little research on Buddha and Zen and here's what I found.

Buddha lived 16 centuries ago, about 563 BC in Northern India or Nepal. He was born a prince. His name was Siddhartha Gautama. He renounced his wealthy life when he found out about the outside world and its suffering. He donned a beggar's robe, shaved his head, and went out into the world on a quest for enlightenment. He traveled the world learning about real life. After his enlightenment sitting under a fig tree, he began to teach. He taught about a path that common people could take to enlighten themselves.

Buddha felt that he could teach people to help themselves instead of turning to a higher being to help them. In his first sermon he spoke of the Four Noble Truths. The truth or acknowledgement of suffering, the causes of suffering, the letting go of suffering and then following the Eightfold Path to become enlightened.

The Eightfold path requires a commitment to wisdom, ethical conduct and mental development. You can definitely apply this to motherhood.

Wisdom - The Realization

• Right view: This is the realization of the four noble truths and understanding that nothing is permanent.

• Right intention: This is a commitment to good will, non-desire and not to act violently.

Ethical Conduct - Getting Started

• Right speech: This is very important. You must choose your words carefully. Words, unlike the old saying, can hurt you.

• Right action: This is to be honest and not do things like lying and stealing.

• Right livelihood: You must take care to gain your wealth by legal means and in a way that will not hurt others.

Mental Development - Putting It Into Action

• Right effort: is the ability to put into practice having the right thoughts, using the right words and doing the right deeds.

• Right mindfulness: is seeing things as they are without judgment. Also, paying attention to the little things.

• Right concentration: Buddhists attain this through meditation.

Zen is a Japanese style of Buddhism. Zen teaches that enlightenment can happen here and now, through experience and based on action.

These simple explanations are just a start to understanding.

There was once a young mother who was lucky enough to study under a Zen Mama. The Zen Mama appeared to have

all the wisdom in the world. The young mother was willing to be a great mother. All she lacked was confidence and experience.

"Zen Mama, help me!" pleaded the distraught young mother. "My children and I are suffering. I am overwhelmed with my job, my housework and all the driving I am doing. I am angry all the time. I have stopped laughing with my children. I need to be a better mother. I don't even know if I'm the same person I used to be." When the Zen Mama said nothing, she began to walk away. When she'd gotten some distance, she heard the Zen Mama call out her name and she turned.

"Young mother, you still turn when I call your name. You are still you. No one truly can understand the warmth of summer without having delved into the depth of winter's cold."

And with that the young mother began to meet with the Zen Mama often.

Chapter One
"Oh Well"

*"If you can solve your problem,
then what is the need of worrying? If you cannot solve it,
then what is the use of worrying?"*
~Shantideva

It's easy to worry about what you can't control. There are so many things to worry about with children:

• Why does my three year-old still need a pull-up at night?

• Why does my four year-old still need his pacifier?

• Why isn't my kindergartner learning to read?

• Will my eight year-old fail the spelling test?

• Is my ten year-old really in love? Is this normal?

• What if my thirteen-year-old makes the wrong decision about where to attend high school?

• Should I let my fourteen year-old start a band with some strange looking kids from school?

• What if my eighteen year-old needs to go to a community college?

Well, your three year old will be trained soon. Your four year old won't have a pacifier in high school. Your kindergartner is really learning but not all five – six year-olds are ready to read yet. Your eight year-old will probably pass next week's test. Your thirteen year-old will decide where to go to high school. If it's the wrong decision, he/she can go to a different high school the following year. Go and meet the kids in the band, do not just decide on the teenager's looks. And, community college _is_ college, you can save money and your child can transfer his/her sophomore year, if he/she wants.

How do we get through these difficult times? It is comforting to know that "this situation didn't come to stay, it came to pass". We all, children and parents alike, grow in the difficult times. When there's something I can't control in my life it helps to say, "Oh well" or "it is what it is!" Let your children be who they are. **Their failures are not a reflection of you. Their successes are not a reflection of you. And they will have both!** And they should.

Letting things go is a difficult concept. I'm up in the middle of the night with some anxiety right now. But I remind myself that life is happening as it is supposed to happen and with that, I'm able to fall back to sleep.

One day the young mother who was perfectly happy with her three year old and his pacifier, began to worry when others began to criticize her. The young mother came to the Zen Mama looking frazzled. "Zen Mama. I don't know what to do. My mother and many other people keep coming to me and telling me that I must take the pacifier away from my three year old. Yet when I do, neither of us gets any sleep at night, which makes the next day terrible! I don't know if I should take it away from my son."

The Zen Mama replied, "Is that so?"

The mother came back a week later looking very happy and told the Zen Mama, "I am so glad I didn't take the pacifier away. We were at a party and my child was able to sleep and everyone complimented me on his wonderful behavior. I'm glad I didn't take away the pacifier."

The Zen Mama replied, "Is that so?"

The next week, the young mother came back and said, "Oh this is terrible, the dentist says that the pacifier will ruin my child's teeth."

The Zen Mama replied, "Is that so?"

The next week the mother told the Zen Mama, "It's so great we had the pacifier on the airplane. The ascent of the plane didn't bother my child's ears."

"Is that so?" replied the Zen Mama.

The next visit to the Zen Mama the young mother was thrilled. "Zen Mama, you'll never guess what happened. When I told my son that we are going to have a new baby, he gave me the pacifier and said, 'I'm all done with this. Let's give it to the new baby.' He hasn't needed his pacifier again!"

The Zen Mama smiled and said, "Is that so?"

The Zen Moral of the Story is: Everything that happens in this life is a mixture of good and bad. Let things go and let them happen as they should. Try to be calm, don't worry.

"If you can't sleep, then get up and do something instead of lying there and worrying. It's the worry that gets you, not the loss of sleep."
~Dale Carnegie

Chapter Two
Pick Your Battles

*"If your heart is a volcano, how shall you
expect flowers to bloom?"*
~Kahlil Gibran

Pick your battles. Mothers have all heard this saying. "Pick your battles" means don't battle everything with a child; pick what really matters to you. Even then, you may ask yourself, why do we still continue to battle so much?

One of the first favorite words of a child is "No!" We used to ask the boys questions, "Do you want a hot dog?" "NO!" Do you want a sandwich? "NO!" And finally we'd sneak in, "Do you want ice cream" "NO!" Then, wait a minute.... "Yes!" They just loved saying "NO!" My brother used to sing the word "NO!" Some kids like it better than other kids. It's powerful! **"YES" is a compliant word; "NO!" means control and power, something kids of all ages love**. (See chapter 5 for more on the secret power of the word yes.)

Small children control their sleep, bathroom skills and eating habits. It gets more complicated with your older children. The battles can be about hair, clothes, bed making, schoolwork, getting up in the morning and whom they hang out with. (This list can go on and on!) The key is to pick some rules that really matter to you and take the anger out of it.

I hardly ever got mad before I had children. I have discovered that anger is so natural! Some children bring out anger you never even knew existed! However, if you're angry all the time, your children will tune you out. Use humor to get your point across. By the way, after you're mad it's ok to apologize and say, "I shouldn't have gotten so angry. I'm sorry." **So often we parents feel that we must be the authority and be right all the time! It's not true. If we teach our children that's it's OK to be wrong and say I'm sorry then hopefully they will be able to do that when they're adults.** After getting mad you also sometimes deal with what I like to call "Parental Guilt". When you say sorry, you often are able to let go of parental guilt, too.

One of the first things I did when I became a "Zen Mama" is try to take the anger out of my life. Last year I would get absolutely furious when I saw a bad grade or a missing assignment. I would explode and think that this would motivate my child. In fact, it had the opposite effect. They would resent me and not try any harder. This year I start out a conversation by saying, "I'm not mad" or "I'm trying hard not to be mad". Then we proceed to have a conversation, not an argument. This is working so much better. And to my amazement my child had a 3.0 last semester. It's working. But I still have to remind myself to take my own advice at least once a week.

The young mother continued to study under the Zen Mama. She came to the Zen Mama and said, "Zen Mama, I am always angry at my children. What should I do?" The Zen Mama gave her a bag of nails and told her that every time she felt angry she should instead hammer a nail into the board. The young mother did this. At first she drove many nails into the fence. After a while, she needed to drive fewer nails into the fence.

*A few weeks later, she proudly told the Zen Mama that she hardly ever drove any nails into the fence any more. So the Zen Mama told her that every time she held her temper she should pull a nail out. Finally, she was able to tell the Zen Mama that all nails had been pulled from the fence. The Zen Mama pointed at the holes and said, "The fence will never be the same. **When you say things in anger, you leave a mark."***

The Zen Moral of the Story: Think before you speak in anger.

*"The world is full of women blindsided by the
unceasing demands of motherhood,
still flabbergasted by how a job
can be terrific and torturous."*
~Anna Quindlen

Chapter Three
Don't Sweat The Big Stuff
(Or The Small Stuff)

*"Let us be of good cheer, remembering that the
misfortunes hardest to bear are those
which will never happen."*
~James Russell Lowell

There is so much to "sweat" about! With many things, you'll find that a year from now, you won't even be worried about it! (You'll have other things to worry about!)

Our culture puts so much pressure on us. The culture says you must fill your children's lives with all sorts of lessons, especially at a young age. Here are some of the things I heard about sports and music activities when my boys were young:

• Are your children in the right soccer/basketball/baseball league?

• If your child doesn't take tennis lessons now (at 6 years old let's say), they won't be able to play in high school.

• Are they in music lessons at a young age?

• Is your baby listening to Mozart?

One of our best summers my children ever had was simply spent digging a big hole in the backyard! We had just read the book, <u>Holes</u>, out loud. We did not do anything organized that summer like tennis or swim team. All the neighborhood kids loved coming to our house to dig the hole that summer.

Find out what they love. If you have a child who loves sports, let him/her fill the summer with the sport. But children actually can start a sport at school later in their young lives and be quite good at it. In fact many children who have taken up a sport at a young age can burn out by the time they're in high school.

My children love to teach themselves new musical instruments. They have luckily had great music teachers at school, too. However, they never wanted lessons and I never pushed that. Since I thought they would never have jobs in an orchestra, I didn't feel the need to push the lessons. All three have thrived as musicians because of their love of music, not the pressure to play and be the best. We are not against music lessons. If they had liked lessons, we would have given them lessons. And now to our surprise, our oldest is now planning a music minor at college.

Besides sports and music, the education of your children also causes much stress.

• Are they reading at the right age? (Often expected at the kindergarten level)

• What are their state and national test scores?

• Is your child in AP classes?

• Are they doing enough homework?

• Kids these days need service projects, good grades and high schools sports and clubs to go to college. My child will never get into college!!

There are so many pressures from school: spelling tests, homework, all the projects that are due when you're all at your busiest. You end up buying poster paper in the middle of a busy evening. If you have a scholar, the pressure he/ she feel to succeed is immense. But not all children are scholars. Then the pressure can be even greater and often just as much for the parents. Yes, your children need to pass but be careful what kind of pressure you put on them scholastically. It might backfire. One of my favorite reading stories is about my oldest son. He had great kindergarten and first grade teachers who didn't believe in pushing reading but believed in giving their students a rich curriculum, filled with art, literature and read aloud books. He didn't read very well until 2nd grade. When he finally did, every book he could get flew off the shelf. He has a love of reading because he did not feel the immense pressure to read.

We have a family story of my great grandparents and their first child. They had an ongoing argument about where he would go to school, Yale or Harvard. The very sad ending of the story is that he died at age five years old in a drowning accident.

Don't sweat the big stuff or the small stuff that hasn't happened yet. I call this my prom syndrome. I came up with it in high school. You can worry everyday for a week that you are going to have a terrible time and you do! That is seven bad days, six spent worrying and one bad time at the dance. Or you can have a great attitude, look forward to the dance and then have a terrible time. That is 6 days of happiness and one bad evening at the dance.

Worry, like anger, is a habit.
There are gigantic issues out there to worry about, like suicide, disease and addictions. The big/small stuff is just that, stuff.

The anxious young mother came to the Zen Mama and said, "I can't sleep for several hours each night. My 5th grader has an "F" on a test. This will bring her grade down to a "C". I'm afraid she'll never pass into middle school."

The Zen Mama replied, "Worry is normal. Situations seems worse at night. Tomorrow is only an illusion. The only reality is today. Today she is in 5th grade. Today she has a bad grade. Everything is unfolding as it should. Do something to make yourself feel better – write your worries in a journal, walk or do some other physical exercise," The young mother wrote her frustration in her journal, but also wrote about all the delightful things she loved about her daughter. After this she felt a little more peaceful and was able to go back to sleep.

The Zen Moral of the Story: Sometimes we are overcome with what the culture says to do. Listen to your children, listen to your gut and try not to worry. Life is happening as it should.

"The central struggle of parenthood is to let our hopes for our children outweigh our fears."
~Ellen Goodman

"Worry often gives a small thing a big shadow."
~Swedish Proverb

尊敬

Chapter Four
Each Child Is Different

*"This is part of the essence of motherhood,
watching your kid grow into her own person and
not being able to do anything about it. Otherwise
children would be nothing more than pets."*
~Heather Armstrong

Have you ever thought to yourself, "I've done all the same things with my second child that I did with my first, but why is he/she so different?" Each child is definitely born with a certain personality. I especially see this in preschool. There are just some girls who were born to wear their fancy velvet dresses each day to school. My son wore a bow tie, even with t-shirts and turtle necks until 1st grade. There are born scientists who live for discussing dinosaurs each day. There are born sports enthusiasts whose whole lives revolve around balls. There are kids who love pink and princesses. There are kids who like trucks and building, others who live for art.

At different times though, I've tried to force one child to be more like the other. I use the word "force" because when it's right and it flows, I'm like a guide bringing all good things together. For instance, I've "forced" the "artistic child" to try a sport that he didn't like at all. What a disaster! I've "forced" music lessons on the "self taught" child who doesn't like lessons. I've "forced" my vegetarian to try new foods that don't fit his tastes. Who do you want them to be, your creation or themselves? I asked my middle son what would he want me to say if I write a book about parenting and he said, **"You are not your children. They are their own person."**

I have really grown to love all the differences in my children; one is an incredible artist, one has a great instinct for sports, and another is quite musical. They all do differently at school depending on the year. At our preschool we say, "What kind of smart are you?" not "How smart are you?" They might be math smart, word smart, art smart, nature smart, body smart, people smart, self smart, music smart or life smart. (These are from Howard Gardner's Multiple Intelligences.) It helps to look at children this way and understand how they look at life.

Besides their interests, you really have to take children's gender into consideration.

Before I became a mother I truly thought children acted more like typical "boys" or "girls" because of how their parents raised them. It's the old argument of nature vs. nurture. But now I know differently!

These may seem like generalizations and not all boys and girls fit. But in general, boys tumble and wrestle and remind me of puppies. They need to move and talk loud. Girls are people pleasers, solving problems through talking. Boys need action. Boys talk when they're shoulder to shoulder. Girls like to face one another. Each gender is motivated differently and has different issues as they go through life. Even their brains are wired differently. Girls have emotion and language in the same area of the brain. In boys, language and emotions are separate. So they are not great are telling you how they are feeling.

Another way girls and boys are different is in the classroom. Girls are often happy to sit, listen and write. Boys usually have more trouble concentrating if they are made to sit all the time and not move, even if it's just a pencil hitting against the side of a desk. Girls like to work in groups; boys like to work by themselves or compete against one another. Girls' hearing is better than boys. So boys shouldn't be sitting in the back of the room where they often do. Even their coloring is different. Boys tend to draw action with a limited amount of color; girls like to draw people with houses and the sun with a lot of color. Certain teachers will be better for one gender than another. Others are learning to change their teaching styles to fit individual genders. Some schools are recognizing this with single sex classrooms.

For more interesting information on gender differences, read Dr. Leonard Sax's book, Why Gender Matters.

The young mother took walks often. She loved walking by water. While she pushed her stroller, her other child rode his bike and they went down a path by a river that she particularly enjoyed. The young mother loved the other side of the river. It made her feel calm. She felt that if she could get her children to the other side of the river that everything would be all right. She often came here when she felt frustrated or troubled. She spent many hours looking at the other side of the river. It was beautiful. The light shimmered in the trees, the flowers were colorful. One day she saw the Zen Mama on the other side of the river. She yelled out, "Zen Mama, how do I get to the other side of the river?" The Zen Mama looked up and down the river and yelled back, "Young mother, you are already on the other side of the river."

The Zen Moral of the Story is: The grass is not always greener on the other side. Do not wish for your children to be something else.

"At first, I saw mountains as mountains and rivers as rivers. Then, I saw mountains were not mountains and rivers were not rivers. Finally, I see mountains again as mountains, and rivers again as rivers."
~Zen Proverb

母亲

Chapter Five
Be A "Yes" Mom

"I hope you're proud of yourself for the times you've said yes, when all it meant was extra work for you and was seemingly only helpful to someone else."

~Mister (Fred) Rogers

Say yes as much as possible. I must give my husband total credit for this idea. His thought was that if you say "YES!" to your children's questions, they are usually satisfied with the answer and an argument is avoided. Now, this doesn't mean that you don't set limits or that there are no rules or discipline. The kids may want to stay up all night or have ice cream before dinner, which everyone knows isn't going to happen. It's just another way of answering questions positively. Often what they are asking never comes to pass, but if it does, you can take care of it at a later date. Try having a "YES!" day or a "YES!" week. Find a way not to say no but to say "YES!" to most everything.

• "Mom, can we go to a movie?"
YES, maybe this Saturday would be good. Instead of, NO we're too busy today.

• "Mom, can we play Go-fish?"
YES, after you clean your room. Instead of NO, I'm cleaning the house.

• "Mom, can I have ice cream for breakfast?"
YES, on your birthday. Instead of NO, that isn't healthy for you'

• "Mom, can we stay up really late tonight?"
YES, on a night that we have nothing going on the next day. Instead of, NO you have a soccer game tomorrow.

• "Mom, can I make brownies?"
YES! Next time I'm at the store I'll get the brownie mix. Instead of, NO, I don't have the ingredients.

There is an exception to putting it off until later.

• "Mom, will you play football/have a tea party with me?"
YES! Right now.   It doesn't need to be long – but **always throw the ball when a child asks, and always have a tea party!** You will never regret it and it will make you feel good, too!

The young mother was very worried. "Zen Mama, my 18 year old son wants to go to Europe this summer, without supervision, with his friend. I don't know how to tell him no, that he is too young."

"Then say, 'yes'. By saying 'yes' you are telling him that you are excited for his plans. Let him dream of the future. If the future works out, then you must consider these plans. But most of the plans of the young are just dreams. Don't take away his dreams"

The young mother came back several weeks later. "You were right Zen Mama. The other boy's parents decided the trip would not happen. We were very sympathetic. Instead we have found a wonderful international camp for him to attend."

The Zen Moral of the Story is: Let your children have their dreams. Say YES and be supportive.

"I thank god for this most amazing day, for the leaping greenly spirit of trees and for the blue dream of sky and for everything which is natural, which is infinite, which is yes."
~e.e. cummings

智慧

Chapter Six

Be In The Moment With Your Kids

*"Do not dwell in the past, do not dream of the future,
concentrate the mind on the present moment."*
~Buddha

Very often your kids don't want to be with you, especially
when they get older. So when they are with you, forget
about what you are doing for a few minutes and give your
children your full attention. It doesn't have to be long, but
at those times, **be in the moment with them.** Act as
though they are the only person you care about at that moment. Make them feel special.

• Don't talk on the cell phone when picking up your kids.
Be in the moment with them.

• When eating a meal together don't answer the phone.
You can call back; meals with kids are often short. Be in
the moment with them.

• When reading a story at night, just do that, read the story. Be in the moment with them.

• When they want to tell you about their day (and that doesn't always happen) or tell you a joke, look into their eyes and really listen. Be in the moment with them.

• The car is a great place to talk, so when in the car, again, listen! It's also a great time to listen to music *they* like. Be in the moment with them.

• When your kids want to play cards, play! Be in the moment with them.

These are just a few examples.

Time is an amazing thing. Nothing else exists when you are in the present moment. Try this, take a deep breath and forget about what just happened, forget where you're supposed to go, forget about what you need at the grocery store, forget when you are going to finish all the laundry. Smile and turn your complete attention to your kids.

Game nights or family dinners are great ways to be in the moment. You can't always have dinner together in this busy life, but there are other ways to be in the present moment. As mentioned above, the car is a great place to talk especially as they get older and don't want to look you in the eye. Don't rush out of the house in the morning. Get up a little earlier so that you can be at the breakfast table to

eat or drink your coffee with them, even if you're not talking and just paging through a magazine; you're still there
with them. Before they fall asleep, peek in and say something positive, as simple as "Sweet Dreams" or "Thanks for
all your help today." **Don't be afraid to just say, "I love
you!"** They may not say anything back but it may also be
an opportunity for them to talk.

You will never be sorry you spent time with your children
when you are reviewing your day. **It's an investment in
your child's future to give them this everyday attention.**

*The young mother and her children were in the house. It
was the second day that the electricity had been out and the
young mother was tired, irritated and her mood was rub-
bing off on the children. Her cell phone was on the last few
cells, so she called the Zen Mama. "Zen Mama, what
should I do? The children are whining, it's too early for
naps and I feel like I can't take it anymore."*

*The Zen Mama said, "As the monk was chased over the
cliff by a tiger, he hung on to a vine to stay alive. While he
was waiting for death, he found a strawberry to eat. It was
the most delicious sweet taste he'd ever tasted."*

The young mother hung up. What did the Zen Mama mean? She thought of the how sweet a strawberry tastes and searched her pantry for something the children would like. She found some chips and candy. They spread a blanket in front of the fire. The children were shocked. Potato chips and candy, not something healthy? "We'll call this an early birthday picnic," said the young mother. They sang each other happy birthday. The kids said it was the best picnic they'd ever had and went easily to their naps.

The Zen Moral of the Story is: Have fun making the most of the moment.

"The future depends on what we do in the present."
~Mathatma Ghandi

"When walking, walk. When eating, eat."
~Zen proverb

Chapter Seven
Send Them To Bed
and To School Happy

*"Sometimes your joy is the source of your smile,
but sometimes your smile can be
the source of your joy."*
~Thich Nhat Hanh

It's so easy to get mad in the morning before school.

You didn't get up. You forgot to make your lunch. Your hair looks bad. Your pants are dirty. Pull your pants up! Where is your backpack? Why didn't you have it ready this morning? Now (after all that) why aren't you talking at the breakfast table?

Well, maybe all these things are true. But you don't have to get mad...these things are true whether you are mad or not.

Don't get mad, choose happiness.

At the end of the day you could be mad, too.

Where is the laundry I asked you to get? Why didn't you do that homework over the weekend? Your room is a mess! Did you bring in the trash cans? Have you walked the neighbor's dog? Now, (after all that) why aren't you telling me about your day?

Well, maybe all these things are true. But you don't have to get mad...these things are true whether you are mad or not. Have a conversation with them without the anger.

Don't get mad, choose happiness.

Make them laugh; make them smile before going to sleep and before leaving the house in the morning. They'll grow up and figure out some of these things. Or maybe they won't. But don't let them go to bed or to school upset or thinking you're mad at them!

The young mother had just finished volunteering at her daughter's preschool. She went to see the Zen Mama later that day, "Zen Mama, I couldn't wait to watch her play with the little dolls in the house keeping room. She's always

talking about them at home. But instead of being a loving girl she got mad at them, put them in time out and suddenly I saw myself through her. Is this how she sees life with me?"

The Zen Mama said, "It's true that sometimes we see ourselves mirrored in our child's play. Maybe you have been angry when you didn't have to be.

The Zen Mama paused and started to tell a story. "Once there was a mother in a boat in a fog. She was worried about getting to the other side of a lake. A boat was heading right for her in the fog. She shouted to the boat to move out of the way. The boat kept coming right for her. She tried several times to get the people on the boat to listen but they kept coming for her. She became frantic and then furious at the crew driving the boat. Soon the boat was upon her and only missed her by a small distance. To her surprise she found that the boat was empty. All the anger she felt vanished, and finally she laughed."

The young mother realized that she shouldn't get angry as often but needed to laugh more in her life with her children.

The Zen Moral of the Story is: When we see a situation that upsets us, we become angry. **Laughter is better than anger,** especially at night and in the morning.

"Man is fond of counting his troubles, but he does not count his joys. If he counted them up, as he ought to, he would see that every lot has enough happiness provided for it."
~Fyodor Dostoevsky

热情

Chapter Eight
Find Out What
They're Interested In

"You need to be aware of what others are doing,
applaud their efforts, acknowledge their successes,
and encourage them in their pursuits.
When we all help one another,
everybody wins."
~Jim Stovall

Find out what your children are interested in. I cannot stress the importance of this enough!

If you have trouble having a conversation with your children, how easy would it be to ask if Pikachu (the Pokeman) and Ash, his master, have ever had a flight with Team Rocket? When my kids liked Pokeman, I read the Pokeman handbook and became a "poke-mom" master. My kids loved it and so did I.

As they've gotten older, I've listened to their music. How nice it is to ask them to explain the lyrics to Vampire Weekend's song, "Mansard Roof". We had fun finding out what a mansard roof is on google. What does the music group Slightly Stooped mean when they write the lyrics of their great reggae songs? Introduce your children to your music as well. We've had great times listening to all my high school music, especially the Beatles. As I mentioned earlier, driving in the car is a great time to make this connection. If they play an instrument, ask to hear them play their music. Listen as if it's the best music you've ever heard. **Music is a bridge between you and your children and as the adult you should attempt to cross it as often as possible.**

I've never known much about sports and I now know quite a bit about baseball and football...and I actually like it! Now, we watch the NFL station and I've learned not only the rules of the sport but many of the player's names as well. I love it!

Here are some starters if you're having trouble with conversation.

• Kids love jokes. Try saying, "Did you hear any good jokes today". (Make sure you have one!) Humor is a sure way to connect. And guess what, you'll feel happier having laughed. It works both ways. (See the appendix for some good jokes.)

• Ask about whom they sit next to at lunch (let's say it's Alex) and then the next day ask, "Well, what did Alex have to say today?"

• Remember what they have told you about and a week later ask how it turned out. My youngest is always coming up with new football plays. I really try to remember them. (Although I'm not always successful!) About a week later I'll say, "Did you try that play that you practiced with Dad...or with the quarterback during practice?" This usually leads to a wonderful conversation.

• The year 2008 was a good year to discuss world issues. If they disagree politically, listen to their opinions and honor them. Sometimes you learn more from those with whom you have opposing views, and that's a good lesson for them to learn as well.

• One of the greatest times to get to know your children is during a family meal. You'll know you're successful when they start telling you about their lives before you have to ask any questions.

If you are in Rome, it's good to speak Italian. **If you are trying to relate to your children, it's good to speak their language.**

One day the young mother and the Zen Mama were sitting, drinking tea.

"Zen Mama, I feel like I don't know my children anymore. We are too busy, even the children, to know what each other is thinking. How do I get to know them again? Can you tell me something of great wisdom?"

The Zen Mama picked up her pen and wrote one sentence: "Pay Attention."

The young mother said, "Is that all?"

"No," said the Zen Mama wrote, "Pay attention. Pay attention."

The young mother became irritable, "That doesn't seem profound to me."

In response, the Zen Mama wrote simply, "Attention, attention, attention."

In frustration, the young mother demanded, "What does this word attention mean?"

The Zen Mama replied, "Attention means attention."

The Zen Moral of the Story is: Pay attention to your kids and in what they are interested. You will be amazed at the results.

"Taking an interest in what others are thinking and doing is often a much more powerful form of encouragement than praise"

"I think it's the great thing about having kids. They have interests that you might not have, and it opens your horizons."
~Robert Martin

"Where words fail, music speaks."
~Hans Christian Anderson

"Part of the fun of being a parent is acting like you don't know anything, so your kids can tell you everything they think they know."
~John H. Henry

Chapter Nine
Let Them Experience Life

"Knowledge must come through action."
~Sophocles

Now, this is a radical idea…**let your children experience life.**

You will want to save them from having the same bad experiences that you have had. But they need to make mistakes because this shapes them into the person they will become.

It is hard to watch them take disappointment; not being chosen for a team, not attending a camp they wanted to go to, a birthday party they missed. One of my children tried out for an international camp. He was chosen to be an alternate. Although he was disappointed, he stuck with the organization. He ended up being selected to go on a trip to Norway. This is very special since our family is Norwegian. He went on to be the junior branch president of the organization.

Relationships in your children's lives will come and go. Friendships will start to become important to children around four or five years old. Sometimes there will be friends that you love and sometimes not. It will often depend on who is in their class. As they get older they will experience the more serious dating relationships. This can be very emotional for boys and girls. Yet, these are the experiences that shape their lives.

Have a plan on how you would like to teach your children about finances in the world. We have taught our children to work for almost everything they have wanted or done in life. We've called this jokingly, "deprivation theory". Since they are rarely given money as a handout, it's amazing how much they appreciate $5.00 for lunch when we drop them off at school and say, "Have a great lunch today!"

Deprivation theory also works in other ways. If you never have certain treats at home, such as sodas or chips, when you do get them it is an extra special treat. I can't tell you how exciting it is when I have a chocolate bar to split among everyone. And when you get 6 pieces instead of three, like my youngest son did just now, it's like winning the lottery!

Our children have paid for part or all of:

• Ski passes and ski equipment
• Ipods
• Trips abroad
• Christmas/birthday presents for their brothers
• Spending money for trips
• Clothing
• Movies
• Cell phones
• Bicycles

We have never allowed them to miss out. We've always helped them if they've fallen short. **They have an incredible work ethic because they have saved and been involved in the money process.** This leads to peace of mind for us as parents because we always know that they will be able to take care of themselves.

Being part of the household is another important responsibility for children. Dinnertime is a great time to get the kids involved. It's also a good time to have them help with cooking, setting the table and putting away the dishes. Even the very youngest can carry his dishes to the sink.

"Zen Mama, I really feel like I am understand this Zen mothering. I am getting close to being an enlightened mother. However, I am still doing so much work around the house and for my children. Is there another lesson I can learn so that our life is smoother and we can have less conflict at our home?"

The Zen mother smiled and said, "Before enlightenment, you chop the wood, you draw the water. After enlightenment, you chop the wood, you draw the water. Perhaps you can enlighten your children and you can chop the wood and draw the water together."

The Zen Moral of the Story is: Sometimes just doing it and experiencing life is the best way of learning.

"Do you know the difference between education
and experience? Education is when
you read the fine print; experience
is what you get when you don't."
~Pete Seeger

"Life can only be understood backward,
but it must be lived forward."
~Soren Kierkegaard

"I have never let my schooling interfere
with my education."
~Mark Twain

理解

Chapter Ten
Nagging Doesn't Work

"You can catch more flies with honey."
~Donald R. Henry

When I was young, I made a promise to myself that I would never be a nag, especially to my husband. I forgot to make that promise to my future children.

Last year, in particular, I found myself becoming a nag. We had all had a very challenging year. When I finally realized it, it was too late! **That's the thing about being a nag; you are as unhappy as the people you're nagging!**

But, where is the line between nagging and a gentle reminder? It's all in the way that you say it. Change the question, "Why haven't you turned in that paper in Math class" (spoken with an angry, exasperated voice) to "Have you checked your grades lately? Let's look at them online and see how well you're doing." Use paper and pencil. Put the good grades and the bad ones on paper. Paper doesn't get mad. Another example: "Why aren't you doing the chores I asked you to do." Put the chores on paper. Paper is telling them what to do, not you.

Also, take the cue from the child. They have been telling you all along, quietly or rebelliously, maybe not even through words, how your nagging is affecting them. So, when you find yourself nagging, ask yourself these things

• What are they good at? Honor that.

• Next, don't compare them with others. Much dissatisfaction comes with comparison.

• Let them talk about it. You might not always like what you hear, but listen.

• Lastly, celebrate that difference. Trust them, and let them learn and go in the direction your child is meant to go.

When I realized that the worst thing failing grades would produce is not graduating and possibly not going to college, I was able to let go and stop nagging. I knew my son would do very well in life whatever happened with his education. Instead of nagging, I let him finally take control of his own education. He's had very positive results this fall semester since I stopped nagging. Great grades...finally!

The Zen Mama and the young mother were walking through an orchard. The young mother was complaining about her daughter and her bike. "Zen Mama, I have taught her since she was young how to take care of her bike. Every time we come home from a bike ride, we wash it off, put oil on the chain and then put it away. But if I'm not there to tell her what to do, the bike becomes dirty. Last time I had to carry her bike off the path because the chain broke since she had forgotten to take care of it. The young mother continued in this vein for a while.

Finally the Zen Mother said, "Young mother, put the bike down."

"What?" asked the confused young mother.

"You're still carrying the bike around. Put it down." replied the Zen Mother.

"You each have your own way of caring for things in your life. The apple trees bear beautiful apples. The pear trees have beautiful pears. Do not nag at the pears to be apples. It's not possible for them. Let them be pears. Besides, our fruit would not be interesting if we only had apples. Find something positive to compliment her about next time you ride your bike together."

The Zen Moral of the Story is: Your child will learn more by watching you than by your nagging.

"I have found the best way to give advice to your children is to find out what they want and then advise them to do it."
~Harry S Truman

"Please give me some good advice in your next letter. I promise not to follow it."
~Edna St. Vincent Millay

友谊

Chapter Eleven
Take An Evening Off

"A happy marriage is a long conversation
which always seems too short."
~Andre Maurois

After all this talk about kids, here is something very important. It's very important to pay attention to your family and friends. Take time off thinking about and talking about your kids, especially with your spouse. We tried this last year on one of our "dates".

At first, you might not have anything to talk about. It's strange how your kids take up all your thoughts. If you can't think of what to talk about besides your children, make a list:

• Are you reading any good books?

• Do you want to see a good movie? (Provides great

discussion after the movie)

• Where do you want to go on our next trip?

• If you could retire anywhere, where would you want to go?

• Tell me something wonderful.

When talking to your spouse you can ask the above questions, but the four questions below lead to great conversation with others:

• Where did you two (husband/boyfriend/girlfriend) meet?

• Where did you grow up?

• What college did you go to?

• What is the most fun project that you're working on?

All of these questions lead to great conversation. You can think and worry about the kids later!

On a rainy day, the young mother came to the Zen Mama feeling a little sad and discouraged. "Zen Mama, my friend and I went out to lunch. We decided not to talk about our children. We found that we had nothing to talk about! It was sad. I realized that all I talk about is my kids."

The Zen Mama pondered this and then asked her a question, "When you came in to my house today, did you leave your boots and umbrella on the porch?

"Yes," replied the young mother.

"Tell me," asked the Zen Mama, "did you put your umbrella to the left or to the right of your boots?"

The young mother didn't know the answer. She didn't know. She had stopped being aware of the little things she did.

The Zen Moral of the Story is: Pay attention to the little things with your friends and spouse. It's good to make your kids your life, but don't forget about the other people in your life.

> *"A baby changes your dinner party*
> *conversation from politics to poops."*
> ~Maurice Johnstone

Chapter Twelve
Teach Kindness

*"No act of kindness, no matter how small,
is ever wasted."*
~Aesop

I don't need to write much here but: Be kind.

If you want to say anything mean to your children, don't. Think of another way to say it. Be kind!

If you want to prove that you are right and your child is wrong, don't. Let them discover it. Be kind!

If you feel like making fun of your child, don't. There is no excuse for this. Be kind!

Be kind. Be kind. Be kind. Be kind. Be kind. Be kind.

By being kind to your children, you teach them to be kind to people in their lives, now and in the future. Also, be kind to yourself; a happy mama is a happy family.

We have so many things to do at home. It's never ending!! Laundry, dishes, dusting, meal planning! There will always be something to do, so take a break. Do it later. You'll be doing it later anyway.

When my two oldest sons were small they would take two naps a day. I would spend the first nap doing all the house-hold chores, getting ready for dinner, paying bills, fighting insurance companies...and anything of importance. The second nap was for me. I'd make a cup of coffee, read, garden, write a letter, work on photo albums. This changed as they got older, but at the time I felt that I was getting things done **and** being kind to myself.

Another way to be kind to yourself is to let go of parental guilt. If there had been a rule book for parenting, we all would have read it many times. We make mistakes and that's OK!

Sometimes we yell at our children. We don't mean to, but we do! The anger, exhaustion and yes, disappointment at them not being the person we believed them to be, builds up and we sometimes explode. Later on or even right away, the guilt sets in. We all do it. Let go of the guilt and start by saying "I'm so sorry."

The young mother said to the Zen Mama, "I am feeling so cranky lately. No one appreciates me; I miss my job where I got a paycheck for work. I'm taking it out on my children. I'm not a good mother."

The Zen Mama then tells her a story about kindness. "A mother was always trying to be a success in life and worried all the time. And felt sad that she wasn't successful in life and that no one appreciated her. One night she had a dream. She dreamt of a fox lying between two rocks with nothing to eat. She waited to see what the fox would do. Suddenly a lion came and gave the fox some food. 'Ah,' the mother said to herself, 'this means I must wait and someone or something will take care of me.' She waited and nothing happened. Then she dreamt the dream again and realized the true meaning. She had to be like the lion, not like the fox.

The Zen Moral of the Story is: When you're feeling this way, find someone who is more cranky or worse off than you are. Help them, be kind to them and it will actually make you feel better, whether it's your children, your husband, a friend or even a stranger. It can be as simple as opening the door for someone or making a family member breakfast in bed. (Even if you felt it should be you having breakfast in bed!)

"Sometimes, all it takes is one kind word to nourish
another person. Think of the ripple effect that
can be created when we nourish someone.
One kind empathetic word has a
wonderful way of turning into many."
~Mister (Fred) Rogers

"I expect to pass through this world but once; any good
thing therefore that I can do, or any kindness that
I can show to any fellow creature, let me do it
now; let me not defer or neglect it,
for I shall not pass this way again."
~Ettiene De Grellet

Chapter Thirteen
Just Love Them

"Whatever they grow up to be, they are still our children, and the one most important of all the things we can give to them is unconditional love. Not a love that depends on anything at all except that they are our children."
~Rosaleen Dickson

Love them, love them, and then love them some more!

Unconditional love is the key. It doesn't spoil anyone. It doesn't mean you can't discipline and set limits. Just take the anger and emotion out. Love them and be unattached to the bad behavior.

When I'm mad or disappointed in my children, I sometimes imagine that something has happened to them. This may sound gruesome but I imagine that they have cancer and their head has no hair, that they're in a wheel chair or worst of all, I'm at their funeral. My eyes will always fill with tears. Then I'll think about what I'm mad or worried about and decide it's not so bad at all!

Another thing I like to do is find a picture of them as a baby or when they're about 5 years old. I remember this perfect, funny, loving baby, child, person my child is. And I see that same person the next time I see them. You feel the same flow of unconditional love for your child that you did when he was a baby. And they feel your love come through.

The young mother came to the Zen Mama and said, "You know what Zen Mama. I think I'm ready to graduate. I think I have learned all your lessons well and I'm ready to mother my children by myself."

The Zen Mama smiled. She knew that you never are finished learning. Even she still had so much learn. She said, "I have one more story to tell you. One day a mother came across a child in the bathroom. The toilet paper was all over the bathroom. She was furious! She had just cleaned up and now the bathroom was a mess. Her young child told her. "Mommy, I'm trying to wrap your Christmas present." Sure enough there was tape and box there, too. Feeling guilty for getting so mad, she helped her daughter finish wrapping the gift and they put it under the tree.

Her daughter couldn't wait for her to open it. A few days later, she couldn't wait any longer. "Mommy, please open my present now." The young mother was in a rush; she couldn't find her keys and they were late to school. She said angrily, "Not now! We've got to go." Then she saw the look on her daughter's face and said, 'Alright but we'll have to make it quick.'

She opened the present and there was nothing inside. Again, thinking about the toilet paper waste, she was quick to anger, "Honey, if you're going to waste all that toilet paper and tape you should at least put a gift inside." "I did Mommy. There are a hundred kisses inside." The mother was again ashamed. She hugged her daughter and realized that she had learned the lesson of unconditional love that day. She would try to hold her anger before speaking again.

The young mother left the Zen Mama that day feeling like life with her children had changed over the year. She had learned to stop worrying and let go. She had become closer to her children in the process. The young mother continued to follow the Zen Mama's suggestions, traveling down the eightfold path. She would continue to make mistakes but the way had became easier.

The most important Zen Moral of the all the stories is this: Just love them.

"And ever has it been known that love knows not
its own depth until the hour of separation."
~Kahlil Gibran

The Appendix

Here are some practical tools to help you along your way as a Zen Mama. Below, you'll find book suggestions, games, websites and of course, the most important mood changer, jokes and riddles.

Great Jokes and Riddles for all ages

3-5 Years Olds
Some great Knock-Knock Jokes, old and new:

• Knock-Knock
Who's there?
Ach.
Ach who?
God bless you!

• Knock-Knock
Who's there?
Choo. Choo who?
I think I hear a train!

• Knock-Knock
Who's there?
Who.
Who who?
I think I hear an owl.

• Knock-Knock
Who's there?
Interrupting cow.
Interrupting cow who?
Moo (make sure you moo in the middle of them
saying "interrupting cow who")

(Don't forget that now you have to listen to abundance of
knock knock jokes that don't make sense. Above all act
surprised when you hear the "orange who" joke.)

6-8 Year Olds

• What's black and white and red all over?
Answers: a newspaper, a zebra with a rash, a penguin
falling downstairs

• Why did Tigger look in the toilet?
Answer: *He was looking for Pooh.*

• Why didn't any dinosaur want to sleep with the Daddy
dinosaur?
Answer: *He was a bronto-snore-us*

• What did the mother broom say to the baby broom?
Answer: *Go to sweep, dear.*

• Where do dogs park?
Answer: *At the barking lot.*

9-11 Year Olds

• What happened at the cannibal's wedding party?
Answer: They toasted the bride and groom.

• Did you hear about the pirate movie?
Answer: *It was rated "agrrrr".*

• Why did the one-handed man cross the road?
Answer: *To get to the second-hand shop!*

• What does a tree do when it is ready to go home?
Answer: *He leaves.*

• A man rode in on Friday and left on Wednesday but only stayed in town two days. How is that possible?
Answer: *His horse was named Friday.*

• Mary had three siblings. One was named Penny, one was named Dime and one was named Nickel. What was the fourth child one named?
Answer: *Mary*

12 Year Olds And Up
Riddles are fun for this group:

• What gets wetter as it dries?
Answer: *A towel*

• I am pronounced as one letter but written with three. Even though you only write my name with two letters. You can read me from right to left or left to right and it's still the same word. What am I?
Answer: *An EYE*

• One day a man was driving home after a hard day's work. He came across a town had been painted black. Everything was painted black; the roads, sidewalks and buildings. In addition, the car's headlights were not working and there was no moon out. Plus there were no street or house lights anywhere. The man came across a solid black dog sitting in the road. Yet he was able to drive around the dog and not hit it. How was this possible?
Answer: *It was 2 o'clock on a lovely sunny afternoon*

• Without me, you would see many people standing in the streets. I can get into places easily without force.
What am I?
Answer: *A key*

• Imagine you are in a room with no windows and no door. How do you get out?
Answer: *Stop imagining*

• I live in a little house, all by myself. My house has no doors or windows. If I want to go out I must break through the wall. What am I?
Answer: *A chicken in an egg*

• A boy was in a car accident with his father. The boy was injured. The father died. The boy was brought to the emergency room. The doctor said, "I cannot operate on this boy; he is my son." How can that be so?
Answer: *It's his mother.*

• You are in a room with no windows and no door. Only a mirror. How do you get out?
Answer: *You look in the mirror, you see what you saw. You take the saw and cut open a hole in the room.*

Dinner Table Games

• The Professions Game
This is a 20 questions game to figure out what job you have. We always start with, "Do you work inside? Outside?" Some great examples: a beekeeper, a wine maker, a zoo employee, the president, and a jockey.

• Say Something Nice Game
Say something nice about the person to your right and then switch and say it about the person on your left.

• Say Something Good You've Done Today Game
Ask everyone to say something nice they have done at
school or at work.

• Trivia Questions
Bring trivia questions to the table to ask the person to your
right or anyone. Or it could be a word that you think no
one knows.

• Message Under the Plate Game
Write or print a different phrase on some post it notes.
Place one note under each of your kids' plates. Make the
sentences a little strange like: "Did I ever tell you I was a
famous movie star?", "It's raining cats and chickens", "I
met the president yesterday at school.", or "I am going to
the moon tomorrow." Before putting food on the plate, ask
everybody to read their sentence under his or her plate, but
do not read it out loud. Use the phrase or sentence in conversation during dinner and see if anyone can guess your
sentence.

• Family Trivia Game
Each of the kids tests the adults with 4 questions.
For example:

What do I usually play at recess?
Who are my two favorite school friends?
What is my favorite class?
What is my least favorite school meal?

Then, the adults test the kids with their own 4 questions. For example:

Where was I born?
Where did I go to elementary school?
Where were my parents born?
In what cities have I lived?

Make up your own questions to continue to learn more about each other.

• What's in the Sock Game?

Have everyone bring a small secret object to dinner. One person begins by hiding a secret object in a clean sock. Pass the sock around the table and lets everyone feel the object. Don't look inside. Everyone takes turns to see if they can guess what's in the sock. The person that guesses right gets to go next.

Books and Websites

Some good "owner's manuals" to read for more ideas and inspiration.

Simplify Your Life by Elaine St. James
Mitten Strings For God by Katrina Kennison
Don't Sweat the Small Stuff With Your Family
by Richard Carlson
Love and Logic by Foster Kline, M.D. and Jim Fay
Why Gender Matters by Leonard Sax, M.D., Ph.D.

Some Great Websites:

www.danggoodjokes.com
www.enchantledlearning.com
www.familieswithpurpose.com
www.zenhabits.net
www.awakeblogger.com

Acknowledgments

I must extend many, many thanks to all the wonderful people in my life.

To all the preschool parents who have passed through Wilder Preschool. I have enjoyed our many conversations. To the teachers I work with, Leslie, Peggy, Julie and Jane, thanks for your friendship; there's not a better team!

To the Henry Family: thanks for loving me like a daughter, a sister and an aunt and not just as an in-law.

To my parents: As Randy Pausch, writer of <u>The Last Lecture</u> writes, "I won the parent lottery." Mom, I'm sure you see your own wisdom throughout these pages and thanks, Dad, for all the edting you've done. I mean editing (JK!)

To my siblings, Philip, Suzie and Andy, there's a quote that sums it up:

"To the outside world we all grow old. But not to brothers and sisters. We know each other as we always were. We know each other's hearts. We share private family jokes. We remember family feuds and secrets, family griefs and joys. We live outside the touch of time."
~Clara Ortega

I also want to thank Peter, Susie and Kim. It's a pleasure to have you in our family. Thanks to my nieces and nephews. I so enjoy your company.

To my aunts: You're like 2nd mothers to me. Or older sisters. Thanks for your confidence and support!

To my children: You've made it possible for me to achieve my childhood dream of being a writer. Thanks for being my inspiration for this book. Thanks for all the wonderful times we've had here and all over the world. Thanks for all your jokes and riddles, too. I love you three so much!

And, the best for last, John. There would no book without you. You helped me so much by saying in the car that day in Boulder, "Just do it!" And I did! You provide support everyday but most importantly you give me unconditional love.

"Being deeply loved by someone gives you strength, while loving someone deeply gives you courage."
~Lao Tzu

Meditation on the Zen Circle

The Zen Circle is a circle made by a single stroke. It does have a beginning and an end yet the circle still goes round, just as life has a beginning and an end. Inside the circle are nothingness, the unknown, and the mystery of all our lives. We don't know what life holds in store for us, today or tomorrow. It is this mystery and nothingness that gives the circle its shape.

梦 想

About the Author

Betsy Henry is a mom, wife and preschool teacher. She grew up in the suburbs of Chicago and went on to get her elementary education degree at Indiana University. She moved to Colorado in 1985 where her family had spent many happy family vacations.

Betsy loves to read, cook, garden and travel with her family. She wrote this book in hope that other mothers will be able to stop worrying, let go and live happier lives. She lives with her husband and three boys in Littleton, Colorado. Please send her a good joke at www.zen-mama.com.

"Your children are not your children. They are the sons and daughters of Life's longing for itself. They came through you but not from you and though they are with you yet they belong not to you."
~Kahlil Gibran

"To Let Go is not to care for, but to care about. To Let Go is not to fix but to be supportive. To Let Go is not to judge but to allow another to be a human being. To Let Go is not to be in the middle of arranging all outcomes, but to allow others to effect their own destinies. To Let Go is not to be protective, but to permit others to face reality. To Let Go is to fear less, and to love more."
~Author unknown

Made in the USA